# Are You Kidding Me?

Jon Coley

Published by Jon Coley, 2023.

ARE YOU KIDDING ME?

**First edition. June 8, 2023.**



ISBN: 979-8223834564

Written by Jon Coley.

For Harper, whose laugh is so wonderful and infectious.

Before you begin, the way this book is organized may be a little confusing. It was originally three different joke books that have now been put together. I didn't want to get rid of the original chapter headings because some of them were jokes too. I just want to make you laugh, not confuse you. After all, that's what parents and teachers are for.

# Chapter One

**In which battles are waged against an octopus and a cardiologist.**

What's an octopus' favorite self defense move?

The sucker punch.

What's bubbly and smells like fish?

Shark farts.

How did the octopus know he took a wrong turn?

It ended up on squid row.

Why did the two by four cutoff have to leave the construction site?

Because it was a little board.

If you're thinking you're going to throw up, just breathe slowly and think about eating sour cream and cat hair. You won't be thinking about much else after that.

Would it be a good idea to take a vacation sometime between April and June?

Maybe.

Why do teachers love apples?

You've got to have some kind of ammo when it all goes down.

Why was the little boy afraid to go to the bathroom?

He just didn't have it in him.

Why is the winged lizard going so slow?

I don't know. He's just a dragon today.

Poodle to Pug:

Your breed is so wrinkly.

Pug to Poodle:

Your breed sounds like it's named after a fart.

What's the difference between homework and farting?

Everybody farts.

The water and ice dispenser is basically the way your freezer goes to the bathroom. Drink up, buttercup!

Your dreams are important, that's why you should stay in bed longer.

Do you have psychic abilities?

No, just not intuit.

Walking around the house with the lights off is dangerous.

There could be a counter strike.

Maybe I should buy a hyperbaric chamber.

I've always thought better under pressure.

I enjoy listening to the radio with frequency.

I got into an argument with a seismologist, but I knew I was on shaky ground.

It's wise to avoid fighting a cosmetologist, because you'll always come out looking bad.

A friend of mine is an entomologist. Sometimes he really bugs me.

I stayed at a hotel during an entomologist convention. Didn't speak a word the whole time I was there, because I knew the place was bugged.

How many entomologists does it take to change a light bulb?

Just one if there's nobody there to bug him.

I was going to tell off my cardiologist, but I didn't have the heart.

Why are they called eagles?

If they swam, they'd be called sea gulls. If they barked, they'd be called beagles.

A friend of mine is a philatelist. He really sticks to what he loves.

A friend of mine is a futurist. I plan to meet her later.

A friend of mine is an optometrist. I always keep my eyes out for him.

What's invisible and smells like oysters?

Otter farts.

Everybody wants to fly like Superman until they have to pick the bugs out of their teeth.

All of you who dislike your legs or think they're ugly, have you ever stopped to consider that you're always looking down on them?

What did the out of breath Aussie say when he saw a dingo chasing a little kangaroo?

Wallaby dog gone!

How many Aussies does it take to change a light bulb?

Just one, but he has to turn it in the opposite direction.

Parent: Do you think money grows on trees?

Kid: Somebody hasn't checked lumber prices lately.

What always has a point no matter how much you argue?

A porcupine.

Never argue with a puffer fish.

They'll just blow up in your face.

This check engine light of mine, I'm gonna let it shine. Let it shine, let it shine, let it shine!

What's a balloon's favorite kind of music?

Pop.

I believe your train of thought has gone off the rails.

Knock knock

Who's there?

Landon

Landon Who?

Landon on your feet is hard to do when you slip on a banana peel.

Knock knock

Who's there?

Mr.

Mr. Who?

Missed her phone call. I'll try again later.

Knock knock

Who's there?

Chris

Chris who?

Christmas is my favorite time of year.

Knock knock

Who's there?

John

John who?

John us at the party. It'll be fun.

Knock knock

Who's there?

Lynn

Lynn who?

Lynn me some money please. I'm broke.

How can you tell if a kangaroo is happy?

It has an extra spring in its step.

Where do royal kangaroos live?

In their bouncy castle.

What did the old tape player say to the new smartphone?

Hey, I'm just keepin' it reel.

I was wondering whether it was safe to go out in the rain. Then it struck me.

I peered toward the east to view the sunrise. Then it dawned on me.

I trained hard for years to become a master mountain climber. Then I peaked.

Why do grown men tell dad jokes?

Because they don't want to get in trouble for telling mom jokes.

Knock knock

Who's there?

Teacher

Teacher who?

Teacher the abc's and she'll learn to read.

I feel sorry for measuring sticks and tape measures. They're rulers, but nobody does what they say.

Every time someone drinks a beer, a bunny dies. It's true. The ingredients say they are made with barley and hops.

Never listen to a baseball player sing in a boat. It's pitchy.

Tractor trailers are great life examples. Especially the way they get hitched and move forward.

I almost got lost in the storm because of cloudy vision.

When one frog asked his friend if his leg was injured, he said, "I hop not."

What should you do if you see a moose? You can always eat it if it's a chocolate mousse.

If it flies and has feathers but no beak, duck! It's an arrow.

Do you like windy places?

No, I'm not a fan.

Knock knock

Who's there?

Almond Joy

Almond Joy who?

Almond Joy-ing this conversation very much.

Knock knock

Who's there?

Yoda

Yoda who?

Yoda man

Nah, Yoda man

Geese get offended if you stare at them too long. They know you're taking a gander.

# Chapter Two

## In which Superman loses his shorts and and farmers go high tech.

If Kal El takes flight too fast and his pants fall down, is that called a super moon?

Knock knock

Who's there?

Cliff

Cliff who?

Cliffhangers are my favorite! Will the door open or stay closed? The suspense is killing me!

Knock knock

Who's there?

Owls

Owls who?

No, owls hoot, but that's an understandable mistake.

Knock knock

Who's there?

Doves

Doves who?

No, doves coo.

Why are roosters so irritable?

I don't know, but I bet it has something to do with all that fowl language.

Horses are so contrary. The only word they seem to know is nay.

Knock knock

Who's there?

Chores

Chores who?

Chores a beautiful day outside.

Why is crime so bad in Australia?

Because all the kangaroos are mob members.

Crime is so bad in the forest because of all the murders of crows.

Rancher Distraught Over Recent Cow Disappearance

Says It's a Big Missed Steak

What did the fox say to the bird dog?

Who do you think you are? Quit hounding me!

Murphy's law was probably decreed from a Murphy bed.

When a woodworker has a tough time fitting a tenon, is that called rigor mortise?

O for goodness sake, unless you're A negative, you should always B positive.

I'd rather be upbeat than beat up. I've always said that.

When someone says, "I'm all ears," I get upset. They're usually nowhere near as ugly as they think they are.

When I hear someone say, "We are short handed today," I wonder how they fish their keys out of their pockets. Do they have to wait until tomorrow?

When you go fishing, you catch fish. But when you go spear fishing, you don't catch spears. That's a shame. Catching spears would be awesome.

The Spanish word for red is rojo, but at Christmas time it's ro-ho-ho-ho.

You sure talk tough for somebody that was in kindergarten five years ago.

Shepherds take care of sheep unless they're German. Then they're guard dogs.

Why do they call it picking your nose? It's not like you're try to choose the best one. You're literally taking whatever you can get. If you're getting a nose job, that's when you're picking your nose.

Knock knock

Who's there?

Doughnut

Doughnut who?

Doughnut do that. You'll get into trouble.

Knock knock

Who's there?

Mistletoes

Mistletoes who?

Mistletoes make it hard to keep you balance when you're walking.

You sure do throw a lot of shade for somebody no bigger than a little shrub.

After the cow jumped over the moon, it was decided that this should never happen again. Hence, ground beef was invented.

Hey diddle diddle,

The cat and the fiddle,

Then he found out what the strings were made of.

The farmer's in the dell.

Agriculture is high tech nowadays.

You talk pretty big for someone who's not even one decade away from the kiddy pool.

If you are under eighteen, you can buy an outfit, but not tobacco products. In other words, that's clothes but no cigar.

If this is a medical emergency, hang up and dial 911. Unless you're jail. This is your only phone call.

HOW TO HAVE A BETTER LIFE AT OTHERS' EXPENSE:

Method #437 - If someone you don't know speaks to you in a funeral home, say, "You can see me?"

HOW TO HAVE A BETTER LIFE AT OTHERS' EXPENSE

Method #374 - The best time to break wind up is when leaving an elevator, especially when others are getting in. Be sure to walk away slowly.

Knock knock

Who's there?

Alpaca

Alpaca who?

Alpaca bag and catch the next train out of town.

Knock knock

Who's there?

Armageddon

Armageddon who?

Armageddon tired of knocking on this door all day.

As a child, the composer got into a lot of trouble. He was always writing notes in class.

The violinist couldn't play for the city orchestra. She was too high strung.

Why couldn't the percussionist play for the city orchestra?

Because of the three-strikes-you're-out rule.

I wanted to play the cymbals in the orchestra, but I don't really stand for anything.

I don't feel well. I feel like Coughing up a fur ball, but I don't like cats.

Did you hear about the chimney sweep epidemic? They all caught the flue.

In science class you learn that honey is bee puke and that number two pencils are tree poop.

I had to break up with my girlfriend for good. She wanted to kiss and make up. I'm perfectly okay with the kiss, but putting on makeup is where I draw the line.

What did the gluteus maximus say to the cerebellum?

No matter what, I'll always back you up.

I think my parents make me check the mail to make me feel better about myself. I'm always finding out that I'm pre-approved and prequalified. I'm like - I know, right?

Knock knock

Who's there?

Tadpole

Tadpole who?

Tadpole needs a flag flying on it. Don't you think?

If someone were to walk a mile in my shoes, he'd experience a lot of confusion - especially after walking into a new room.

English is hard. In the word, FOOT, the two O's make the the short U sound. But change the F to a P, and they make the long U sound. The only thing these two words have in common is that they both really stink.

Knock knock
Who's there?
Peanut
Peanut who?
Peanut there, for 'tis not yon bathroom.
Knock knock
Who's there?
Keith
Keith who?
Keith are on the drether, I think.

Knock knock
Who's there?
Heath
Heath who?
Heath not here yet, tho I'll come back later.
Knock knock
Who's there?
Radio
Radio who?
Radio the old bus driver finally retired last week.

If you're buying used paint, be sure it comes from a house similar to yours. Or else, you'll never get it to fit.

If you're ever feeling sorry for yourself, just remember that you can jump higher than an elephant. Elephants don't jump.

This math problem is more confusing than a sewage leak in a chocolate factory.

# Chapter Three

**In which space aliens are addlepated and two states are viewed.**

Knock knock

Who's there?

July

July who?

July too much. I can't believe a word you say.

My mom couldn't go to church because of Ernie.

Who's Ernie?

Ernie hurts every time it rains until she puts ice on it and props her leg up for a while.

What did the six-legged insectoid space aliens say to the human race?

We come in peace. As you can see, we are unarmed.

What did the soda addicted, confused space aliens say to the human race?

Take us your two liters.

This is my favorite suit because I earned it.

How did you earn it?

I earned it nice and slow so it wouldn't have any wrinkles.


Knock knock

Who's there?

Beth

Beth who?

Beth you can't count to theven in Thpanith.

Knock knock

Who's there?

Arkansas

Arkansas who?

Arkansas it, but will Tennessee it too?

Q: How was your weekend?

A: Sunday morning I had to go to the hospital.

Q: You already got out?

A: The doctor told me it was just a case of Saturday Night Fever.

I've been learning to cook Soul Food.

So far it's been meaty okra.

Why did the chicken cross the road?

To get away from all the other hens' fowl language.

Knock knock

Who's there?

Mr. Potato Head

Mr. Potato Head who?

Mr. Potato Head by a mile. Should've aimed for her watermelon rear end.

The Pilsbury Dough Boy was rushed to the hospital.

He got his hand caught in the cookie jar.

Knock knock

Who's there?

Aunt Jemima

Aunt Jemima who?

Aunt Jemima just the nicest lady I ever met? You're a lucky kid.

I think the Manwich hand ought to go into thumb wrestling. He would be the all time world champion. No one would be able to put their whole body into a match like him.

Knock knock

Who's there?

Popcorn

Popcorn who?

Popcorn I have a drink of water? I'm really thirsty.

Knock knock

Who's there?

Celery

Celery who?

Celery furbished tablet for half price, and I just might buy it.

Knock knock

Who's there?

Shirley

Shirley who?

Shirley you recognize the sound of my voice.

Knock knock

Who's there?

Jose

Jose who?

Jose can you see by the dawn's early light?

(Yeah, I know. Too easy.)

What did the flat tire say after the wreck?

This is too much for me. I need some air.

I wore sneakers to school, but everybody still knew I was there.

Knock knock

Who's there?

Disney

Disney who?

Disney hurts, but dat knee's okay.

Lumber: I'm board.

Drill: I'm boring.

Nail: Shut up. I have a headache.

The eyes are windows to your soul, and apparently your nose is the window to my business.

Your mom's so random she disappeared for a week when the squirrels got into your attic.

Knock knock

Who's there?

Batman

Batman who?

Batman over there is from my hometown.
Knock knock
Who's there?
Batgirl
Batgirl who?
Batgirl with him is really cute.
Knock knock
Whose there?
Two Face
Two Face who?
Two Face the world takes courage, but I believe in you!
Knock knock
Who's there?
Penguin
Penguin who?
Pen Gwen with a fine quill, and you'll have a beautiful signature.
Knock knock
Who's there?
Superman
Superman who?
Soup her, man! The customer is always right. And give her some crackers too.
Knock knock
Who's there?
Water
Water who?
Water name is, I really couldn't say.
Your mom's so wrinkled she uses a dryer sheet in the shower.
People who run anti-bullying campaigns could use a punch in the face. (Maybe I shouldn't put this one in the book.)
Jam is always better than jelly, except for toe jam.

If you ever see Dracula descending a staircase, do not follow him. You wouldn't want to be down for the count.

Did I just see you petting a tree?

Yes, it was a fir tree.

Teacher: You see, class, oil is extracted from other things. Sunflower oil comes from sunflower seeds. Corn oil comes from corn ... Oh no, why are you crying?

Student: I'll never use baby oil again!

Knock knock

Who's there?

Cousin

Cousin who?

Cousin is a bad habit. Perhaps you should wash your mouth out with soap.

Would you like a sandwich?

I don't know. Is she a good witch or a bad witch?

If there be any among you who do not like vegetables, speak now or forever hold your peas.

If there be any among you who need to go to the bathroom, speak now or forever hold your pees.

The truth is, if you want to be clean, you must first believe in the lye.

If you decide to walk a mile in someone's shoes, make shirt it's a round trip, because ... no shirt, no shoes, no service.

The thing about those people who would give you the shirt off their back is that you can't take them anywhere. No shirt, no shoes, no service.

Cars pass gas all the time, but when I do it, people are suddenly offended.

The board to the screw: Okay, let's get to work. You know the drill.

Why did the vegetarian eat alone?

He wanted some peas and quiet.

In many animals, the females are cows and the males are bulls. But not possums, because that would be a possum bull.

(Wow, that was a long way to go for a bad pun.)

# Chapter Four

## In which a conversation becomes a fart joke. Don't they all?

Student: If beans are so good for you, then why do they make you fart?

Teacher: Who said farting is bad for you?

Student: You mean farting is good for you?

Teacher: Sure, it's just bad for everybody else.

If you're not sure how to use a power drill, just watch the hole video.

Self conscious people usually avoid going into skyscrapers. It's because of all the stairs.

Seamstress: (Nonchalantly) Sew what?

What did the sleepy cat say?

Nothing. He was catatonic.

Why are elevators so grumpy?

Because everybody's always pushing their buttons.

If you're going down an escalator, is that deescalating the situation?

It's hard to be friends with elevator operators. One minute they're up, next they're down.

If you ever feel that life is unfair, remember this. If something is about to hit a duck in the head, there's nothing you can say to warn it.

Knock knock

Who's there?

Cock-a-doodle

Cock-a-doodle who?

No, silly, it's cock-a-doodle-do.

You may think I'm snarky, but that's just how eye roll.

Teacher: You're very propitious, aren't you?

Student: Of course I am. Who doesn't like peaches?

Laughter is the best medicine, until somebody pees. It's hard to say what the best medicine is after that. Depends.

Let's face it. Both guys and gals can be total pains in the rear end. They're not called him-her-roids for nothing.

It was such an irony that the dry cleaner didn't impress me.

What did the moss say when the old tree fell?

I'm lichen what I'm seeing.

Knock knock

Who's there?

Robin

Robin who?

Robin banks is illegal. Just thought you should know that.

EVER SINCE THE DENTIST PUT CAPS ON ALL MY TEETH, I CAN'T STOP YELLING. I DON'T KNOW WHY!!!

I wrote a book on bears. Barely escaped with my life. Should've written it on paper.

I don't care what anybody says. Gluten free spaghetti isn't real. It's an im-pasta!

Our teacher, Mrs. Reynolds, likes to sing hip-hop karaoke. It's fun to listen to Mrs. Reynolds rap.

Knock knock

Who's there?

Giraffe

Giraffe who?

Giraffe at me? I raff at you! Ha ha ha.

I got caught behind a bread truck in a traffic jam the other day. Oh, the irony.

The other day I heard that the department store had their pants half off. I'm not going in there.

Bakers have anger issues. They're always beating their eggs.

Statistically speaking, shark attacks are very rare. Makes sense to me. I've never once attacked a shark.

In the US, there have been zero unprovoked wolf attacks in the past one hundred years. That makes sense. I can't imagine a wolf ever doing anything to provoke me to attack it.

They say people drink more milk than cows. I totally believe it too. Can you imagine how exhausting it would be to try to drink a cow?

What did the lead singer of the Mighty Mushroom Band yell out at the beginning of the concert?

Hey Hey! It's time to party with the fungi!

Why can't a mandolin be in a guitar band?

It's too high strung.

Teacher: Just keep working until you finish.

Student: That'll be a really long time. I'll always be Swedish.

Me: My new friend is very interesting. She's Swedish.

Other Friend: She's pretty Saltish if you ask me.

Nobody: Do you eat with your right hand or your left?

Me: I usually eat with a fork.

At the store I saw a sign that read, NO PUBLIC RESTROOM. Hats off to them I say. In his day and age, there's just no sense in going to the restroom in public.

Why wasn't the stork feeling well?

It had a frog in its throat.

What did the other stork say about it?

See, I toad you so.

Your mom's so dumb, if she were a fish, she'd drown.

Knock knock

Who's there?

Tom Sawyer

Tom Sawyer who?

Tom Sawyer mom at the beauty shop today, but she didn't look any better.

Knock knock

Who's there?

Loofah

Loofah who?

Loofah-Rig-No is the best Hulk ever, and that Mark R. Buffalo is probably green with envy.

Knock knock

Who's there?

Fern

Fern who?

Fern the hole - take cover!

Knock knock

Who's there?

Chip

Chip who?

Chip in if you want me to stop making knock knock jokes.

You may be confident, but you'll never be - dog sniffing its own butt in front of people - confident. This is mostly because you probably can't reach, though.

Picking your clothes is like picking your nose. It's usually done at home alone, yet everyone knows how good you are at it.

Kids, don't be too judgmental when your teachers make bad decisions. After all, they decided to work with you on a daily basis.

Little Boy: Grandma, why do you keep looking out the window?

Grandma: I'm just enjoying watching the birds frolicking in the birdbath.

Little Boy: Oh, I suspected fowl play.

When the weather cools and it's time to turn on the heater, half a year's dust is burned off the coils. Dust is mostly human cells, so you are literally inhaling seared human flesh. Just one more reason why I love Halloween!

(On the playground.)

Student: God, it's cold!

Teacher: At least you're talking to the right person.

Student: Of course we have PE on the day I'm wearing jeans.

Teacher: It'll be all right. I've had PE in my jeans before.

Student: Might want to get that checked out.

Teacher: Maybe ... Depends.

Why do French people eat escargot?

The don't eat fast food.

I don't think my plumber likes his assistant. He whole time they were working I kept hearing, "Hand me the pipe dope."

Why did we decide to "drive" cars like we "drive" screws and "drive" nails? It's like we had catastrophe on our minds right from the beginning.

# Chapter Five

# In which the book comes to an abrupt end because

Knock knock

Who's there?

Wendy

Wendy who?

Wendy you think you'll get around to opening this door?

It's time to feed my pet duck his favorite snack - quacker jacks.

He also likes peanut butter and quackers.

For breakfast, he likes quacker instant grits.

By the way, my jokes really quack him up.

All I'm saying is that they stopped paddling kids in schools and now young people walk around with their pants drooping halfway to the ground. It can't be a coincidence.

Knock knock

Who's there?

Shower

Shower who?

Shower grade be an F or an F minus? That is the question.

The idea of going to City Hall is enough to give you nightmares. But don't worry, the day time mayor's office hours are from nine to five.

And now ... the reason you'll probably regret buying this book. It's time for the KNOCK-KNOCK-A-TORIUM!

Knock knock

Who's there?

Lettuce

Lettuce who?

Lettuce begin

Alice

Alice who?

Al is our master of ceremonies

Hummus

Hummus who?

Hum us a tune and let the festivities begin

Principal

Principal who?

Prince Ipple and Prince Apple will be joining us soon.

Avery

Avery who?

Avery body put your hands in the air!

Blue

Blue who?

Blue up the bouncy house. Let's get hoppin'!

Red

Red who?

Red the instructions, but they didn't make sense.

Yellow

Yellow who?

Yellow, nice to meet you.

Calculus

What? You've got to be kidding.

Yeah, I'm totally kidding. Nothing goes with calculus.

Kid 1: Did you know that I can jog faster than a car?

Kid 2: No way! That's impossible.

Kid 1: Sure I can. Cars don't jog.

Kid 1: I can jump higher than an eagle.

Kid 2: No you can't!

Kid 1: Sure I can. They're only a few feet tall.

Kid 1: Why are you spitting so much?

Kid 2: Can't get the grit out of my teeth. Our teacher told us to turn in our papers face down.

Kid 1: Once upon a time, there was a kid who had a pet cow.

Kid 2: Oh no.

Kid 1: He named it Dora.

Kid 2: Please don't.

Kid 1: Later on he discovered it was actually a boy.

Kid 2: And here it comes.

Kid 1: But it was still adorable.

Kid 1: Why don't woodworkers like to carry too much at one time?

Kid 2: Not again.

Kid 1: They don't want to be embarrassed by dropping their drawers in front of everybody.

Kid 2: You need to get a better hobby.

Kid 1: I just wrote a book on buffaloes.

Kid 2: I can't do this anymore.

Kid 1: It was a lot of work.

Kid 2: I'm not listening. I'm not listening.

Kid 1: Next time, I'm totally going to write on a computer.

Kid 1: My dad hired a tree surgeon yesterday.

Kid 2: Come on, don't go there.

Kid 1: I was amazed that a tree could even become a surgeon.

Kid 2: I need to get some new friends.

Kid 1: We went to the dog trainer yesterday.

Kid 2: I don't like where this is going.

Kid 1: I didn't even know a dog could become a trainer.

Kid 2: Yup. I don't like where it went.

Kid 1: Well, we had to retire the old family car yesterday.

Kid 2: Oh, are you going to get a new or used car?

Kid 1: Why would we do that after put four new tires on it?

Knock knock
Who's there?
Soda
Soda who?
Soda pressed you won't open the door.
Kid 1: My dad decided not to buy that new saw after all.
Kid 2: Why me, Lord?
Kid 1: It was a tough decision, but it just didn't make the cut.
Kid 1: My family took a road trip through Kansas and Ohio last weekend.
Kid 2: Can we please just not?
Kid 1: We took plenty of pictures.
Kid 2: This isn't happening.
Kid 1: Unfortunately, they were all too grainy.
Kid 1: I have a pen pal from Nebraska.
Kid 2: No one has pen pals anymore.
Kid 1: He's a nice guy, but he's really corny.
Kid 2: I'm glad that's over.
Kid 1: Well, we talked on the phone a couple of times too.
Kid 2: Oh no.
Kid 1: It was hard to understand him, though.
Kid 2: Why am I still here?
Kid 1: It could have been the connection, but he sounded really husky.
Kid 1: I have to eat one serving of yogurt at every meal nowadays.
Kid 2: I gonna regret this. Why?
Kid 1: My mom wants me to be more cultured.
Kid 2: Yup, I totally regret it, and now I need an antibiotic.

Kid 1: I read a little of one of my sister's vampire romance novels the other day.

Kid 2: I've gotta go.

Kid 1: It was okay, but the main character really sucks.

Kid 2: Like your jokes?

Kid 1: What?

Kid 2: What?

Kid 1: I just found out how to make a small fortune playing video games.

Kid 2: Really? How?

Kid 1: Simple. You just start out with a large fortune.

My dad wanted to take the family to Sweden this year, but I told him Norway Jose.

The trip to Norway was fun, but the transportation was uncomfortable. All they had were fjords.

Why does Lucy always pull the football away before Charlie Brown can kick it?

Because he would never even bother to kick a baseball.

I used to date a confectioner. That one was a real sweet talker.

Just came out of a long term bittersweet relationship. What can I say? Chocolatiers.

Why is the number 10 so stressed?

Because it's always caught between a 911 emergency.

Your mom's so mean that if you look up mean in the dictionary, her picture's NOT there, because they didn't want to make her mad.

Kid 1: My uncle is a lumberjack.

Kid 2: Here we go again.

Kid 1: Sometimes he talks to the trees.

Kid 2: Worse than I thought.

Kid 1: He says stuff like, "You know what this axe is for?"

Kid: And here it comes.

Kid 1: Of course, the trees don't answer.

Kid 2: Because they were totally stumped!

Kid 1: No, because trees can't talk.

Why does Schroeder have a bust of Beethoven on his piano?

Because the real Beethoven is dead.

Why does Lucy charge a nickel for psychological therapy?

Because advice from a kid isn't worth a dime.

Why does Linus carry a security blanket around with him?

Because security guards are too heavy and expensive.

Kid 1: The other day, I took some video of a mallard.

Kid2: Okay, why?

Kid 1: Because my dad ask me to bring him some duck tape.

Your mom's so skinny and bucktoothed she won't go in a hardware store for fear of being mistaken for a rake.

# Chapter 1A

**Funnier that a bunch of clowns climbing out of your family car on a dark, stormy night.**

Kid A: You know, people really rush to judgement when it comes to all of the other reindeer.

Kid B: What makes you say that?

Kid A: I'm just saying that they would have let him play all the reindeer games if he were nice Dolph.

Kid A: Did you hear what happened at the circus?

Kid B: No, what?

Kid A: A tumbler got dropped.

Kid B: Oh no! That's terrible.

Kid B: Well you know, just couldn't carry the water.

Knock knock

Who's there?

Gemini

Gemini who?

Gemini are going to the movies. Would you like to join us?

What's the ugliest kind of plant?

A face plant.

Kid 1: We had a good time on our tropical vacation, but some of the palm trees looked depressed.

Kid 2: How can a tree be depressed?

Kid 1: Yeah, I thought it was kind of weird too, so I looked it up.

Kid 2: Okay, what did you find out?

Kid 1: It turns out they were face palms.

Kid 1: I'll tell you what. That self help book I've been reading is worthless.

Kid 2: Do tell.

Kid 1: It gives stupid advice, like how to be less lazy next week.

Kid 2: I don't follow.

Kid 1: I'm not being lazy next week. I'm being lazy right now.

Kid 1: I've given up playing video games for good.

Kid 2: Wow, what happened. We were just playing together online last night.

Kid 1: I just changed my mind. Now I'm playing video games for evil.


Kid 1: I just quit cold turkey.

Kid 2: Quit what?

Kid 1: Cold Turkey. From now on I'll only have hot turkey.

Kid 1: I know a guy who hates ghosts.

Kid 2: Why does he hate ghosts?

Kid 1: Don't know. I guess he's just a wraith-ist.

Knock knock

Who's there?

Water

Water who?

Water you talking about?

Knock knock

Who's there?

Water

Water who?

No, Napoleon met his Waterloo, not his water who.

Kid 1: Did you hear about the man who was charged over a million dollars by the postal service?

Kid 2: No. How did that happen?

Kid 1: Well, that's what happens when you address the elephant in the room.

Kid 1: What do you call chili that isn't crooked?

Kid 2: I don't know. What?

Kid 1: Keep thinking. You'll figure it out even chili.

Kid 1: I wanted to go hiking with a friend of mine the other day, but he couldn't because of issues?

Kid 2: what do you mean?

Kid 1: Issues are too tight when he puts on his favorite socks.

Kid 1: I'm feeling a little low today.

Kid 2: Why's that?

Kid 1: It's all mathematics. If just two hundred thousand people would give me five measly dollars, I would be a millionaire. Too bad people only think about themselves.

There once was an old, thick, raggedy rope. It worked on the wharf, mooring boats to the docks. One day, it decided to go to a swanky restaurant, because it heard they served an outstanding string cheese dish. Unfortunately, when it sat at the table, the waiter said, "We don't serve your kind here."

The old, raggedy rope left the restaurant dejected. However, it decided to try something. It looped, wiggled, and got itself completely tangled. Then it went back into the restaurant and sat at the table. The same waiter came to the table and eyed the rope suspiciously.

"Let me guess," said the rope, "You don't serve my kind here."

The water said, "A coarse knot?"

# Chapter 2A

## So funny, you'll throw up in your mother's shoes.

Kid 1: I've finally decided what I want to do with my life.

Kid 2: Do tell.

Kid 1: I'm going to buy a locomotive and paint it my favorite color, gun metal gray.

Kid 2: Great idea.

Kid 1: There's more. I'm going to name it after my grandfather, Victor. I'm going to use the most luxurious cars available, paint them gray, and stamp my logo on each one, a great big V.

Kid 2: Wow, you've given this a lot of thought.

Kid 1: Sure I have. Everyone will want to ride the gray V train.

Why do people like deer so much?

Because they're all hart.

(You see, hart is an archaic term for deer, and jokes are so much funnier when you have to explain them.)

What's invisible and smells like rotten fish?

Cat farts.

I think the reason that electric car races aren't a thing is because the competitors would be called e-racers.

Why won't anyone trust leopards?

Most people suspect they're cheetahs.

Kid 1: For his New Year's Resolution, my dad had sworn off grapes.

Kid 2: Why would he do that?

Kid 1: Oh, he has his raisins.

Kid 1: My aunt was dating a woodworker, but she had to break up with him.

Kid 2: Why?

Kid 1: She said he had too many vices.

Kid 1: The lab results finally came in yesterday.

Kid 2: Is everything ok?

Kid 1: Sure, there were five healthy puppies in all, three boys and two girls.

If the time is the hour between one and three, does that make a clock two faced?

Kid 1: My uncle has a weird habit.

Kid 2: I'm shocked.

Kid 1: Yeah, I know, but this is what he does. When he's eating, he closes his eyes just before he takes every single bite.

Kid 2: That's pretty weird, alright. Why does he do that?

Kid: I don't know, but he's always hated seafood.

Hats off to all you London limeys, especially the ones whose jobs are on the street close to Big Ben. You literally work around the clock.

Kid 1: There was an owl in my backyard last night.

Kid 2: I bet it kept you up a while if you heard it.

Kid 1: Yes, saw whet too.

(This joke would be hilarious if you were an ornithologist, because a saw whet is a species of owl. And of course, jokes are so much funnier after you explain them.)

What did the blanket say to the sheet?

Don't worry. I've got you covered.

Kid 1: I made fish stew.

Kid 2: Sounds good. How did it turn out.

Kid 1: It wasn't easy. They aren't what you call the touchy-feely type.

Kid 2: Say what?

Kid 1: Now I've made you stew too.

Kid 1: I made deer sandwiches last weekend.

Kid 2: Well, that sounds different.

Kid 1: I know, right. The deer just scampered away every time I got close, though.

Kid 1: My crazy uncle got kicked out of our kitchen the other day.

Kid 2: Uh oh, why?

Kid 1: He was making dog biscuits.

Kid 2: That's a little strange, I guess.

Kid 1: The local pet shelter thought so too.

You shouldn't be afraid to try new things, especially the ones that aren't my patience.

I was considering purchasing twelve dozen eggs, but that would be one gross order.

(Again, this is funny to those of you who know that one gross is equivalent to twelve times twelve, or one hundred forty-four. So if you didn't laugh at this joke, at least you learned something.)

# Chapter 3A

# You'll cackle like a witch stirring a bubbling cauldron of mimes' feet.

Kid 1: Dad just got back from Florida.

Kid 2: Did he have a good time?

Kid 1: It was a business trip, but he did get to go to a racetrack.

Kid 2: Did he win big?

Kid 1: No, he picked a horse named Charles.

Kid 2: Was that a bad pick?

Kid 1: Oh yes, I'd never run with a Charlie horse in Miami.

(Okay, this one really is funny. Say the last line out loud. If you don't think that's funny, I can't do anything for you.)

Algebra, like all math, is really problematic.

I would tell you a joke about language arts, but it's really wordy.

Knock knock

Who's there?

Office

Office who?

Office rocker he is. I tell you, he's crazy.

Kid 1: Hey, your cat looks like he's depressed.

Kid 2: Yeah, it looks like a bad case of meows-ma.

Two men were having a conversation, but only one was doing all the talking. The other gentleman just stood quietly, holding a goose under each arm. After the two men parted, the gentleman with the birds started calling back to the other man over his shoulder. At first this confused me, but hen I figured out what was going on. When ya speak, port ya geese.

Knock knock

Who's there?

Column

Column who?

Column what you want. They still look like rows to me.


Knock knock

Who's there?

Courtney

Courtney who?

Courtney-ds to take a small recess, because the judge needs to pee.

(Yeah, I'm a little ashamed of this one myself.)

Teacher: How many feet in a yard?

Kid: I don't know.

Teacher: I'll give you a hint. It's an odd number.

Kid: Well, that's no fair. You should have told us that there'd be pirates involved.

(I'll admit, I didn't get this one when I first reread it. But come on, it's hilarious me hearties.)

Kid 1: Hey, I heard you had to switch work groups in science class.

Kid 2: Yeah, it was for the best. They were studying electrons.

Kid 1: So what?

Kid 2: I just couldn't be around all that negative energy.

Kid 1: Why did the chicken cross the road?

Kid 2: I heard it was because she saw a rooster in a field of beautiful wild flowers.

Kid 1: Sounds like poppycock to me.

Why do bulls have only two horns?

Because the cows have all the udders.

Wiseman: Hello, my child. What knowledge do you seek?

Disciple: I must purchase a plant for my wife, as she loves them greatly. But she is so particular about her clothing, never allowing even a speck of dust upon them. What should I do?

Wiseman: Fear not. You must buy her a cactus.

Disciple: Why a cactus, oh wise one?

Wiseman: You must buy her a cactus, because it is a succulent. Then you can tell her, "It will succulent right off your clothes."

Disciple: Oh wise one, is not true that two wrongs do not make a right?

Wiseman: Yes, it is not true.

Disciple: I do not understand, oh wise one.

Wiseman: Would you not say that something is wrong if there is a law <u>suit</u>?

Disciple: Most certainly.

Wiseman: If the government has a <u>case</u> against you, would not something also be very wrong?

Disciple: Very wrong indeed, oh wise one.

Wiseman: Yet, my child, when you put them together, you get a <u>suitcase</u>, which means you are going on a vacation, and there is nothing wrong with that.

Disciple: I think I could use one now.

Wiseman: What?

Disciple: What?

How many buglers does it take to change a light bulb? Nobody knows. The more burglars in the house, the darker it gets.

Why did the king go to the bathroom in the middle of a poker game?

Because nothing beats a royal flush.

(Yeah, that's right. I've got potty humor.)

# Chapter 4A

## You'll giggle more than I did when I heard those jokes about your mom.

Knock knock

Who's there?

A soldier

A soldier who?

A soldier bike to your neighbor for a hundred bucks. You're welcome.

Knock knock

Who's there?

Letter C

Letter C who?

Letter C is important, so practice your reading skills.

There were three leopards and a man in an enclosure. One of the big cats went and sat by him. Why did leopard A and leopard B stay away from the man? Because he had leopard C.

Kid 1: Did you have a good time at the zoo yesterday?

Kid 2: Sure. There were kangaroos, hippos, and we even spotted some leopards.

Kid 1: Wow, I'm surprised they didn't bite you.

Kid 1: My mom told me I had to take an origami class.

Kid 2: What did you do?

Kid 1: I could tell she meant business, so I folded.

I wanted to learn how to make glue, but I couldn't stick with it.

Kid 1: I'm a little disappointed with my new math tutor's attitude.

Kid 2: Uh oh, why's that?

Kid 1: We were working in subtraction, and she just kept saying, "What's the difference?"

The sun was surprised that he was in middle of the solar system. He didn't planet that way.

Knock knock

Who's there?

Baxter

Baxter who?

Baxter your seats, face the front and pay attention, class. This isn't recess.

Kid 1: Did you finish your book report?

Kid 2: No. Eclipse.

Kid 1: There wasn't an eclipse yesterday, was there?

Kid 2: No. My little brother, eclipse too many pages from my book for it to make sense.

Knock knock

Who's there?

Thomson

Thomson who?

Thomson is a nice kid, but May's son is kind of a jerk.

Knock knock

Who's there?

Mason

Mason who?

May's son heard we were talking about him.

I feel sorry for floors. People think they can just walk all over them.

I feel sorry for doormats. They're always treated like a ... Ohhhh, I get it.

Public Service Announcement:

Please support hardwood dance floors.

Sincerely,

PATUCOR

People Against the Unnecessary Cutting of Rugs

We shouldn't wonder why people have trouble following instructions. I mean, we would think someone was crazy if they took off their shoes when told to wipe their feet. Would we not?

Knock knock
Who's there?
Empress
Empress who?
Empress me and I'll think about taking you with me.
Knock knock
Who's there?
Oliver
Oliver who?
Oliver friends say she's great, but I don't know her very well.
Knock knock
Who's there?
Beverly Clearly
Beverly Clearly who?
Beverly Clearly, without a doubt, loved writing.

I'm not saying that you have a bad mom, but Starburst also comes in orange, strawberry, and cherry flavors.

# Chapter 5A

## Funnier than an octopus on roller skates, if you're not an animal rights activist.

Knock knock

Who's there?

Daughter

Daughter who?

Daughter eyes and cross her tees - that's what she needs to do to get a better penmanship grade.

Kid 1: What did the chicken say when it crossed the road?

Kid 2: I don't know. What?

Kid 1: Nothing. Chickens don't talk.

Why did the chicken cross the road?

It had it coming.

Kid 1: I'm planning on starting an aviary.

Kid 2: That sounds expensive.

Kid 1: Not at all. I already planted all the birdseed yesterday.

What do you call a dishonest digit?

It's a cheat toe.

Kid 1: My cousin had a meltdown the other day.

Kid 2: Why? What happened to him.

Kid 1: He was walking his dog, and someone accidentally stepped on its paw. Then he just freaked out.

Kid 2: That's terrible!

Kid 1: What can I say? It was his terrier of some kind.

Kid 1: I saw a scary movie last night.

Kid 2: Did it have an axe murderer in it?

Kid 1: No, he only murdered people, except for one girl.

Kid 2: How did she get away?

Kid 1: She was running from the bad guy, and he tripped over some briars. She lived due to the vine intervention.

Knock knock

Who's there?

Burrito

Burrito who?

Brrr it oh so cold out here. Please let me in.

I decided not to go back to yoga class. I just can't stand being around all those posers.

Knock knock

Who's there?

Spaulding

Spaulding who?

Spaulding a little, but he could always do a comb over.

Knock knock

Who's there?

Aloe Vera

Aloe Vera who?

Aloe, Vera smart of you to find out whoever's knocking before you open the door.

How many math teachers does it take to change a lightbulb?

Just one, but it takes a really long time, because they always have to show their work.

Kid 1: I'm worried about my uncle. He needs to gain some weight.

Kid 2: Oh no! Is he sick?

Kid 1: No. He converted from Catholic to Protestant, so he has no mass.

Knock knock

Who's there?

Razor

Razor who?

Razor hand if you think knock knock jokes are funny.

I need to stay put and think about my health. It's a weighty decision.

Knock knock

Who's there?

Summer

Summer who?

Summer saying that you will never open this door. I'm beginning to believe them too.

Knock knock

Who's there?

Winter

Winter who?

Winter you think I should give up and quit knocking?

Kid 1: My mom and dad are arguing again.

Kid 2: What's the problem?

Kid 1: We've been working on our lawn. Dad had me picking up rocks and putting them in a bucket.

Kid 2: That's no fun.

Kid 1: No, but he gave me bonus with my allowance.

Kid 2: Okay, so why are your parents arguing?

Kid 1: Yesterday, I filled a whole bucket up with rocks. My dad said that I could fill up another bucket by going farther back into the yard. My mom heard this and got mad. She yelled, "That's way beyond the pail!"

(And that, kids, was a lot of work for one punchline.)

Kid 1: My dad said something cool the other day, so I paid him a quarter.

Kid 2: Was it worth it?

Kid 1: Sure, I coined the phrase.

# Chapter 6A

# Just as funny as any joke book YOU'VE ever written.

Knock knock

Whose there?

Frazier

Frazier who?

Frazier words carefully while speaking in public. They could come back to bite you.

Knock knock

Who's there?

Senior

Senior who?

Senior friend the other day, He says hi.

Knock knock

Who's there?

Gauze

Gauze who?

Gauze who what?

What?

Gauze I said so?

A carpenter was working on a commission for his client, Mr. Wynn. Before going to the job site, he asked his kid to help him load some materials into the work truck. The child held up a decorative sconce, and asked his father what it was. He told him, "Oh, that's just Wynn's sconce, son."

Knock knock

Who's there?

Walnut

Walnut who?

Walnut believe it til I see it with me own eyes!

Knock knock

Who's there?

Kenny

Kenny who?

Kenny do it? Yes he can!

Kid 1: Hey, did you hear about Johnson?

Kid 2: No

Kid 1: Yesterday at the track meet, he ran the forty in five flat. Yesterday at the track meet, he ran the forty in five flat.

Kid 2: Great! Why did you say it twice?

Kid 1: It's a broken record!

(Music was once played on spinning pieces of vinyl called records. If a record were scratched or otherwise broken, the needle would bounce causing repetition. Once again, explaining your jokes makes them supper funny.)

Why do elderly people have so much trouble with falling?

It's because they've outgrown their legs.

In fact, most elderly people still have two kidneys.

Knock knock

Who's there?

Tequila

Tequila who?

Tequila Mockingbird is an American classic. You should read it.

And I shouldn't wine about it either.

That's the spirit.

Knock knock

Who's there?

Avocado

Avocado who?

Avocado cold, so it's a little hard for me to talk right now.

Kid 1: My family had dinner at that new restaurant last night.

Kid 2: You mean the one that has corn and grain based dishes from different cultures?

Kid 1: Yup. They call it CORN-FUSION.

Kid 2: Wow, it sounds A-MAIZE-ING.

Why did the dairy cow not want to walk out into the pasture?

Her calves were killing her.

Who called it the chicken dance instead of a fowl ball?

Knock knock

Who's there?

Gruesome

Gruesome who?

Gruesome of those bell peppers you like in my garden. Come on over.

A customer notices that a cashier's name tag says NOBODY.

"I like your name tag," he says.

"Thanks," she says, "Our boss said that nobody deserves a raise."

(This was a true story, by the way.)

Knock knock

Who's there?

Summer

Summer who?

Summer there's a person who will open the door when I knock. I just know it.

Knock knock

Who's there?

Tinkerbell

Tinkerbell who?

Tinkerbell is broken. What do you think?

Knock knock
Who's there?
Frazier
Again? Frazier who?
Frazier your bread so that it won't go bad too soon.

# Chapter One B
# The Snarky Teacher Said
# (These are snarky, but not belittling comments that will make a kid's day.)

You should always endeavor to be studious and well behaved. After all, you're not going to be able to get by on your looks.

I didn't give you a bad grade because I don't like you. I had the lunchroom lady spit in your soup for that.

Either your imaginary friend is sitting on your lap, or you're texting in class.

Long distance relationships are difficult, like the one you'll soon be having with recess.

Roses are red. Dookie is brown. Time for you to hush and sit yourself down.

Silence is golden. So are boogers. Choose wisely.

Either you're trying to achieve a one cheek sneak, or you're looking at your friend's paper. Both scenarios seem pretty stinky to me.

Rules are meant to be broken, just like your little pencil neck.

You talk pretty big for a kid who doesn't know the Spanish word for taco.

Good news! You're no dumber today than you were yesterday.

My years of work experience and top notch educator training more than allow me to declare with utmost confidence that your domestic canine most certainly did not consume your homework.

Math is magical. It makes my students cry.

Good news! You're no uglier today than you were yesterday.

Guessing is like sneezing. You should only do it when necessary. Doing it to much will lead to a snotty result.

Being upset about getting a bad grade after not doing your homework is like picking your nose and being surprised there's a booger on your finger.

Guessing is like pooting. Doing it too much will lead to a stinky situation.

For some of you, I can tell that passing a test will be like passing a kidney stone.

Listening to kids is like hugging a cactus. You know you probably shouldn't do it. Then you do it. Then you realize how stupid you were.

Coming up with the perfect lesson plan that entertains and interests you while promoting good learning is very difficult. Making you work your fingers to the bone is a piece of cake, and you know how much I like cake.

The key to being smarter is for you to think about what you were going to say, then don't say it.

# Chapter Two B
# Winter Safety Tips

Remember, as long as you have ice sickles, you have a weapon. And when it melts, so does the evidence.

Never trust a yellow snowman.

If you feel the need to make snow angels, don't do it in a dog park.

It's fun to catch snowflakes with your tongue, but the birds are always watching.

If it's too cold outside for you, setting your hair on fire won't keep you warm for too long.

It's important to learn cursive. For one thing, it's makes it much easier to pee your name in the snow.

If a snowman has a lemonade stand, don't buy it. Lemons don't grow in the winter time.

If you want to keep your snowman from melting too fast, put some clothes on it. But not yours. You won't enjoy playing in the snow naked.

Remember, if you want to hug a polar bear, be sure you don't smell too delicious.

Don't be too prideful. Everybody smells like carrots to a snowman.

Don't pick up a snowball you didn't make yourself. You may be in a snowman's bathroom.

I find it highly suspicious that no one knows what snowman poots smell like and it's always windy in winter.

Skiing uphill is pretty much always stupid.

If you're ever hungry in the winter, never eat a polar bear's liver. It has so much vitamin A and that it will kill you. Besides, the polar bear won't give it to you anyway.

What's invisible and smells like a cold winter wind? Snowman farts.

My mom told me to put on a jacket, but I didn't. I have the right to bare arms.

Why won't snowmen talk about their feelings?

They're as cold as ice.

What's the last thing a snowman wants to hear you say?

Hi there!

# Chapter Three B
# Summer Survival Tips

You can only make yellow snow angels in the summertime.

If you get a bad sunburn, just wrap yourself in toilet paper and say you're going to a costume party dressed as a candy cane.

If you get too hot, go act stupid in front of a teacher so you can get a cold stare.

If someone swims to the far edge of the pool to be alone, he's probably peeing.

There's no better dance teacher than the act of walking barefoot across a sandy beach in the summer.

If you walk your pet pig down the street on a hot summer day, it will smell delicious in no time.

If you're worried about drowning during a summer thunderstorm at night, just wear floaties to bed.

If you feel like you need to lose some weight, just sit outside in a skimpy bathing suit. The mosquitoes will take care of the rest.

If you're swimming in the ocean and a shark attacks you, just play dead. It won't help you, but at least you'll get a head start.

# Chapter Four B
# St. Patrick's Day

Why do leprechauns have pots of gold?

Because it won't fit in their wallets.

Why do leprechauns have pots of gold at the end of the rainbow?

Because they can't keep them in the middle of the rainbow. It's up in the air.

Why do leprechauns wear green clothes?

Because otherwise they'd be naked.

Why did St. Patrick drive all the poisonous snakes out of Ireland?

Because snakes can't drive.

Why did St. Patrick drive all the poisonous snakes out or Ireland?

It was before the Scottish invented golf balls.

Why shouldn't you keep a four leaf clover in a book?

You'll be pressing your luck.

Why do you have to catch a leprechaun by the heel to get his gold?

Because you might fall in and get wet if you catch him by the creek.

Why didn't St. Patrick drive all the leprechauns out of Ireland?

They had plenty of gold, so they could pay their own way.

# Chapter Five B
# Random Jokes

What did CS Lewis say when asked about his inspiration for THE LION, THE WITCH, AND THE WARDROBE?

"It's Narnia business."

Remember, order matters. For instance, toilet paper is a great idea. But paper toilet, not so much.

Do cannibals eat pizza with their hands?

No, they usually like them just fine without it.

Remember, tissue paper and toilet paper are only interchangeable before time of use.

Why would an Italian baker chase you down the street?

To tell you that you focaccia bread.

If see your injured foot, I may get sick. I'm black toes intolerant.

Why do the bride and groom cut the cake during the wedding?

Because it would be rude to cut the cheese.

How can you tell if your friend's lost his marbles?

He doesn't have any.

Daily hygiene is so important.

No one wants to have a louse-ee day.

What do you call a dyslexic surgeon?

Doctor, if you live through the procedure.

Why did people stop using feather beds?

Because they were always feeling down.

Why is the Easter Bunny so poor?

He kept all his eggs in one basket.

How many librarians does it take to change a lightbulb?

Just one, but it takes a long time, because they have to use the Dewey Decimal system.

What do you call an elderly person who puts out fires?

A firefighter - what is your problem with old people, anyway?

Why can't you trust a vacuum cleaner?

It's been gathering dirt on you.

What do you call a blonde person who drives a truck?

A truck driver. Now you're picking on blondes.

Why doesn't the yellow brick road go through Georgia?

Because you couldn't find it, much less follow it, in the spring time.

What sound does a brontosaurus make.

None. It's dead.

Why are doors so funny?

They're always good for a knock knock joke.

I went target practicing and in the fog today.

I mist.

Why are fires so unhealthy?

Because smoking is such a bad habit.

Why are rocks so easy to be around.

They're just so down to earth.

I used to have an eel skin wallet, but it was a real pain in the backside.

Why do librarians envy police officers?

Because they get to throw the book at people.

My librarian told me that my book on abnormal psychology was in. She said it was crazy.

The librarian said that the book about angels was heavenly.

When I asked for my book about gossip, the librarian said she heard it was fantastic.

I asked the librarian if she had any books on paranoia. She said, "Why, what have you heard?"

Why was the professional wrestler kicked out of the bakery?

Because he kneed the dough too hard.

My librarian said that my book on Irritable Bowel Syndrome wasn't your regular kind of read.

My librarian said that the book on cattle ranching was a mooo-ving experience.

Why did the bakery have to close?

They didn't make enough dough.

Me: Say Goon.
You: Goon.
Me: Say loon.
You: Loon.
Me: Tune.
You: Tune.
Me: What do you eat people with?
You: Spoon.
Me: What? You eat people?
Is this the year they finally find Bigfoot?
Not Yeti.

I just found out my wallet's made of eel skin. I was shocked.

Adult: It looks like you grew three feet since last year.

Kid: No, I only have two feet.

What was the first homework assignment ever?

When God told Adam and Eve to go forth and multiply.

When a librarian goes fishing, what does she use for bait?

Bookworms!

Standards are like family. You may have them, but you don't want to meet them every day.

Why do scientists use beauty products, like blush and foundation?

It helps them to make up their minds.

Why did the bully throw a lamp at someone?

Because he needed to lighten up.

Why did the auto mechanic visit the art museum?

He wanted to see the van go in person.

I was shocked when I found out my electrician was unlicensed.

I find it ironic that stoop is poots spelled backwards, because when you stoop, that's what you do.

# Chapter Six B
## Vegetation

Why is it a waste of time to talk to flowers?

Because they already have all the anthers.

Why are flower fields so peaceful?

Because every flower has a pistil.

If plants were political, they'd have a yellow flag. It would be a pollination.

Why don't cucumbers like salt or vinegar?

Because they don't want to be in a pickle.

He tried to sell me an old pickle jar, but I thought it was a bad dill.

Why aren't people afraid of trees?

Because they're all bark and no bite.

Why won't secret agents accept flowers?

Because they could be a plant.

Why shouldn't you trust a tree?

Because you'll end up out on a limb.

Why should you always watch what you say in the Midwest?

Because there are thousands of ears in a cornfield.

2 for 1

What did the tree say to the thunderstorm?

You blow me away.

What did the thunderstorm say to the tree?

You're all wet.

What did the thorn say to the briar.

Thistle do just fine.

What did the bird say to the cactus?

I'm in a sticky situation.

It's just a little cruel to mow your lawn in front of a vegetarian.

How many vegans does it take to change a lightbulb?

Only one if he can stop talking about being a vegan.

What did the flower say to her offspring?

You're growing like a weed.

# Chapter Seven B
# Halloween

How many zombies does it take to change a light bulb?

Just one if he still has his arms.

What's a zombie's favorite party snack?

They love finger foods.

Why do ghosts always try to be truthful?

Because they know we can see right through them.

Why won't ghosts try Chinese food?

They don't have the guts.

Why are ghosts considered a tough crowd?

Because they're always booing.

Why do spirits lack confidence?

Because they know they don't stand a ghost of a chance.

What's the best way to write scary stories?

Hire a ghostwriter.

How can you tell if your neighbor's a werewolf?

Look out you window at night to see if you can catch him peeing on your shrubs.

What did Frankenstein's monster say to his psychologist?

I'm barely holding it together.

What did the mummy say to the psychologist?

I feel like I'm coming undone, but I really need to unwind.

Why were the ancient Egyptians so crazy?

They had a lot of mummy issues.

# Chapter Eight B
# If you can't say anything nice ...
# Tell a good 'Your Mama' Joke.

(Disclaimer - Be careful with these. Your Mama Jokes can be a lot of fun at the right time in the right place with the right people. Kids love their mamas, though. Sometimes the only worse fighting words than Your Mama Jokes are, "You wanna fight?")

Your mama's so ...

Crazy - she tried to use the remote control to change her mind.

Ugly - she waxes her beard with Crisco.

Dumb - she stopped paying for your washing machine because the salesman said it would pay for itself in few months.

Fat - she saved us all from a meteor crash because she has her own gravitational field.

Loud - the neighbors almost died because they couldn't hear the tornado siren.

Dumb - she cooks meatballs to watch Spaghetti Westerns.

Fat - she was placed under house arrest because she couldn't fit in a jail cell.

Scary looking - a ghost tried to give her its sheet so it wouldn't have to look at her.

Big - I had to go back three episodes on my binge watching after she walked past the TV.

Stinky - the pest control company hires her out when they need to fumigate.

Ugly - contractors hire her to scare old paint off the walls.

Cheap - she pours Animal Crackers in milk for your breakfast cereal.

Dumb - she winks when she's making a turn to give the blinker moral support.

Fat - when she said she was so hungry she could eat a horse, she started a stampede.

Nutty - she only eats jelly sandwiches.

Ugly - she has to be buried in a time capsule to get her beauty sleep.

Bossy - the grocery store checkout machines won't talk to her.

Tall - when people say she's got her head in the clouds, it because it's true. HER HEAD IS IN THE CLOUDS!

Short - she wears high heels in the roller coaster line.

Dumb - she went to a quarry to listen to rock music.

# Chapter Nine B
# Animals

What did the mother panda say to her mischievous cub?
   I can't bear your bad behavior.
   What did the cat say about the missing canary?
   Nothing, his mouth was full.
   What did the rams say when all the females began to wander off?
   Ewes better get back here!
   Why do people love baby kangaroos?
   Because they're always a Joey to be around.
   Why do dogs always follow you to the bathroom?
   Well, we always watch them when they go.
   Why don't dogs like Cajuns?
   Because they're always eating hush puppies.
   Why can't you trust the king of the jungle?
   Because it's always a lion.
   Why won't anybody share secrets with rodents?
   Because they don't want to be ratted out.
   What's a shark's favorite light snack?
   Hush guppies.
   It's a bad idea to keep camels and cows in the same pin.
   It's way too much dairy drama for the dromedary.
   (My wife gave me this one.)
   Why do farmers put bells on their cows?
   So they can keep time while playing their horns.
   If a bear were to come into your living room, where would it sit?
   Where ever it wants.
   What do you call a June bug in December?
   Dead.
   What did the water buffalo say to her clumsy calf?
   I musk ox you to be more careful.
   Why do fish swim in schools?
   They like being graded on a scale.
   Snakes are so unhelpful. They literally can't give you a hand.

Why is it so fun to play with orcas?

Because you're sure to have a whale of a time.

Why was the dolphin so anxious?

He needed to find his porpoise in life.

Why was the puppy put on a special diet?

Because he was a little husky.

Why do geese have to fly everywhere they go?

Because they're such rude drivers. They're always honking at everybody.

Why don't people ever pay attention to fish?

Because everybody knows they're all wet.

The scuba diver encountered a nest of eels.

It was a shocking experience.

Me: My pet fish is special. It can breathe underwater!

You: How's that supposed to be special?

Me: You can't breathe underwater, can you?

How many birds does it take to screw in a light bulb?
Most can't even do it, but the toucan.
What is a cow's favorite greeting?
Hey there.
Counselors don't like working with turtles. It's too hard to get them to come out of their shells.
I'm not sure that X-raying the dog is a good idea. Perhaps CAT scan.
If a group of kangaroos is called a mob, is a flash mob a group of dancing kangaroos?
Why are some farmers wary of sheep?
They can be quite wooly from time to time.
If dogs could fish, what would they catch?
Catfish.
What do you call a really talented sea creature?
A starfish.
A goat was jaywalking. The traffic officer yelled, "Hey, stop ewe!"
Why couldn't the pony make a speech?
He was a little hoarse.
What happened to the frog after he ate a bad fly?
He croaked.
(Come on, you should've seen that one coming.)
What did one spider say to the other?
Better check your fly.
Why won't llamas talk to camels?
They can't get over the hump.

# Chapter Ten B
# Knock-Knock Jokes

(Full disclosure - I hate knock-knock jokes. Either I really love my readers, or I really hate myself.)

Knock-knock
Who's there?
Ilene
Ilene who?
Ilene over to pull up my socks.
Knock-knock
Who's there?
Alfred
Alfred who?
Alf read the book, but he didn't like it.
Knock-knock
Who's there?
Jolene
Jolene who?
Joe, lean over and pick up that trash please.
Knock-knock
Who's there?
Alabama
Alabama who?
Alabama this nail with my hammer until I drive it all the way in.
Knock-knock
Who's there?
Joe
Joe who?
Joe mama said to stop telling bad knock-knock jokes.
Knock-knock
Who's there?
Homer
Homer who?
Homer was hit to tie up the game.

Knock-knock
    Who's there?
    Bart
    Bart who?
    Bart I don't want to hear anymore bad knock-knock jokes.
    Knock-knock
    Who's there?
    Canopy
    Canopy who?
    Canopy in your bathroom? I've really got to go!
    Knock-knock
    Who's there?
    Wilma
    Wilma who?
    Wilma ever stop talking about the good old days?
    Knock-knock
    Who's there?
    Tommy
    Tommy who?
    Tommy this is the best book ever! How is it to you?
    Knock-knock
    Who's there?
    Theo
    Theo who?
    Theo gray mare isn't what she used to be.

Knock-knock
Who's there?
Washington
Washington who?
Washington, teeth, and the rest of your mouth is good hygiene.
Knock-knock
Who's there?
Sheba
Sheba who?
Sheba the last pair of shoes in the shelf.
Knock-knock
Who's there?
Andrew
Andrew who?
Andrew a beautiful picture, that's what he did.
Knock-knock
Who's there?
Amy
Amy who?
Amy the arrow is the first step in target practice.
Knock-knock
Who's there?
Jessie
Jessie who?
Jessie that over there? Neat, isn't it?
Knock-knock
Who's there?
Vera
Vera who?
Vera difficult it is to come up with good knock-knock jokes.
Knock-knock
Who's there?

Sunday
Sunday who?
Sunday my prince will come.
Knock-knock
Who's there?
Olive
Olive who?
Olive just around the block from you.
Knock-knock
Who's there?
Ida
Ida who?
Ida bet a million dollars you don't know my real name.
Knock-knock
Who's there?
Annie
Annie who?
Annie said his name was Ralph.
Knock-knock
Who's there?
Abe
Abe who?
Abe bout time you let me come in.
Knock-knock
Who's there?
Billy
Billy who?
Billy for the rest and I'll pay you later.
Knock-knock
Who's there?
Willy
Willy who?

Willy or won't he? That is the question.
Knock-knock
Who's there?
Ashley
Ashley who?
Ashley, I've always preferred puns to knock-knock jokes.
Knock-knock
Who's there?
Juan
Juan who?
Juan a go to the store with me today?
Knock-knock
Who's there?
Dinosaur
Dinah's sore after her hard workout.
Knock-knock
Who's there?
Collier
Collier who?
Collier mom and tell her to come to the door.
Knock-knock
Who's there?
You
You who?
No, that's a delicious chocolate drink.
Knock-knock
Who's there?
Wendy
Wendy who?
Wendy you plan on opening this door?
Knock-knock
Who's there?

Amanda
Amanda who?
Amanda man conversation is going to have to be had about this.
Knock-knock
Who's there?
Water
Water who?
Water you doing on the other side of that door?
Knock-knock
Who's there?
Sharon
Sharon who?
Sharon time with you is always fun.
Knock-knock
Who's there?
Jackie
Jackie who?
Jackie car up before changing the tire.
Knock-knock
Who's there?
Wyatt
Wyatt who?
Wyatt, red, and blue are patriotic colors.
Knock-knock
Who's there?
Tourist
Tourist who?
Tourist after a long days work is a wonderful thing.
Knock-knock
Who's there?
Tupelo
Tupelo who?

Tupelo zero is mighty cold.
Knock-knock
Who's there?
Mandy
Mandy who?
Mandy you believe how many knock-knock jokes there are in this book?
Knock-knock
Who's there?
Coelacanth
Coelacanth who?
Coelacanth believe it either.
Knock-knock
Who's there?
Scott
Scott who?
Scott you too? I hope we can get away!
Knock-knock
Who's there?
Xavier
Xavier who?
Xavier self! There's no hope for me.
Knock-knock
Who's there?
Banana
Banana who?
Banana and their little brother, Mike, are all coming over to play.
Knock-knock
Who's there?
Chucky
Chucky who?
Chucky dirty clothes down the stairs so I can wash them.

Knock-knock

Who's there?

Dawn

Dawn who?

Dawn thine armor, my lord. The battle has begun!

Knock-knock

Who's there?

Dr. Seuss

Dr. Seuss who?

Dr. Seuss comedian for making people laugh so hard that they were in stitches.

Page

# Don't miss out!

Visit the website below and you can sign up to receive emails whenever Jon Coley publishes a new book. There's no charge and no obligation.

https://books2read.com/r/B-A-OVTX-VSDKC

BOOKS 2 READ

Connecting independent readers to independent writers.

Did you love *Are You Kidding Me?*? Then you should read *Skate or Die Jacob Jones*[1] by Jon Coley!

Skating Sensation Jacob Jones has come to Sierra Vista...

To support the troops, he's putting on a show ...

But something is wrong. In fact, everything's gone bananas. Join Jacob as he skates through a town plagued with chimpanzees, skunk apes, good old fashioned zombies, and copious amounts of banana pudding.

Now a Firebird Book Award Winner!

Read more at www.joncoleyauthor.com.

---

1. https://books2read.com/u/bPLDxd

2. https://books2read.com/u/bPLDxd

# Also by Jon Coley

Schooling Abraham
Schooling Abraham
Tickled to Death: Funny Epitaphs for Kids
Numbskulls: Navigating Personality Conflicts
Anthology of Seasons
Skate or Die Jacob Jones
The Not So Great Divide
The Echo Chamber
Are You Kidding Me?

Watch for more at www.joncoleyauthor.com.

# About the Author

Jon Coley lives in Georgia with his wife, daughters, an orange cat, an eccentric husky, and an overly affectionate a Great Dane. He has been a school teacher for more than two decades.

Read more at www.joncoleyauthor.com.

# About the Publisher

Jon Coley is dedicated to providing poetry and fictional prose for middle grade readers.

www.ingramcontent.com/pod-product-compliance
Lightning Source LLC
Chambersburg PA
CBHW051901130726
47987CB00002B/929